Recipes from a Teenage Chef: Easy meals for independent young adults

PLUS Great Tips for Eating & Living a Healthy Life.

By
Christian Kelly
www.Christian-Kelly.com

Dedication

First of all, thank you to God, for His limitless blessings, and for all that He has done, and continues to do for me. I love you.

To my mother, Carla Melissa Kelly, who passed away the day after I was born- I know you continue to watch over me, your light shining down on me day after day. Without you, I would not be here. I love you, and in time, I will see you again.

To my parents, Christopher & Julette Kelly, without you guys, this project would not have been possible. You guys have been such a blessing in my life, and I thank God for you both. I wouldn't be half the person I am today, if it had not been for you both. You both had a major part in my desire to cook and become a chef. Every time I would try something new, you were there to give me your honest feedback. Every time I wanted to make Sunday dinner, you never hesitated to go out shopping for what I needed. Thank you for always pushing me to do my best and wanting nothing less than excellence for, and from me. I thank you for the love that you show me every day, every hour, every minute, and every second. I love you guys with my whole heart.

To my Granny, Aunt Paula, Aunty Nikki, Aunty Jenny, and Aunt Tara, you guys played a big part in making this happen, and you don't even know it. You are the reason cooking is my passion, and you don't even know that. Since I was a little kid, I always used to watch you guys cook and wanted to be a part of it. You are the lit match that started the fire for this passion that I have. I love each and every one of you, and I can't thank you enough.

But maybe unlimited family discounts at my future restaurants can be a start.

Special Dedication: To my Pastor, Dr. Therman E. Evans. I can honestly say that my life would NOT be the same if you were not in it. You have impacted me and my family's life in countless ways; you've encouraged me, your words of wisdom have guided me, and the love you and Lady B have shown me, has forever changed me. May God bless you, in all the days of your life; I love you both.

Table of Contents

Introduction

Hey there - my name is Christian Kelly. I'm 19 years old, and if you haven't figured it out by now, I have a thing for cooking. I love food. Food makes me happy, it's my passion. I enjoy being funny and making people laugh. It's a part of my personality I really like. I just love seeing people happy. And cooking does just that for me. It allows me to make people happy by making something that appeals to their taste buds, therefore putting a smile on their face.

I mainly come from two different backgrounds: Guyanese and Nigerian (which explains why I like to use different spices). Both Guyanese and Nigerians are known for enjoying spicy food. But if you don't like your food spicy, don't worry; my recipes are not made to be hot. Honestly, I'm not a big fan of hot and spicy foods, but if you are you can always adjust the spice level to your taste.

Ever since I was about 5 years old, I've had an interest in food, other than eating it. I guess it was due to the fact that I've been exposed to cooking for as long as I can remember. Whenever my Grandmother or Aunts were cooking, I would always find myself in the kitchen either helping or simply watching. They were like my "Rachel Ray" of the day. One other thing I can remember to this day was, when my brother, sister, parents and I moved into our new home in Jersey, those first couple years, we ALWAYS cooked. I mean, on a nightly basis. My Dad was pretty much the chef of the house, he was the one to do most of the Sunday cooking, the *fancy* dinners, and there have been plenty of times when I had to ask him "where did you learn to cook" because *everything* he made, I was impressed with, I kid you not.

But what stuck with me the most was when we used to all be in the kitchen together, as a *family,* all preparing dinner. My Mom and

Dad were the "Head chefs", my brother and sister like the "Prep cooks", making salad and whatnot. And me? I was the audience. Just standing by, watching, observing. Gradually, I went from being the audience, to "Prep cook", to "Sous Chef" to one of the "Head Chefs" (of the kitchen).

(Really quickly, I must mention one thing. At this point in the book, you've seen me mention things about "my mom." Let me clarify. My biological mother did pass away the day after I was born. But ever since my Uncle and his wife stepped into my life since I was a kid, I've always considered them my parents, so I refer to them as my "mom" or "dad" or "parents". Just so there is no confusion). Okay, now back to what I was saying!
Another thing we always did together was play music while we cooked. So, you would have all five of us in the kitchen, cooking, talking, laughing, and having an honest *family moment*. Those memories I will **never** forget about. Actually, listening to music while we cooked is what really got me to start singing, and now it's pretty much a routine for me. Every time I'm in the kitchen, I always listen to music and sing.

Let me tell you something that happened before I even knew how serious I was about cooking. Years ago, my family and I went camping with a group in Canada for about a week. There was a lady there named Mrs. Erika, and she was a "chef" in my eyes, because she seemed to really enjoy feeding people. She cooked some meals for the families, just because she wanted to, and everything she made tasted really, really good. Well, I would always like to stand by and observe her as she cooked, and I guess she took note of me watching her, because one day she says to my mom:

"Your child has a serious relationship with food. I wouldn't be

2

surprised if he was to get into that field when he grows up."

Now mind you, this was BEFORE I realized that I had a passion for food, and cooking beyond my childhood desire and curiosity. She named it before I fully realized it myself.

She was most certainly right.

That passion started to grow when I started collecting cookbooks, and watching cooking shows. That's when I really started to become serious about cooking. In high school, I decided to take a culinary class my freshman year. And I loved it! I went on to complete the next two courses, making it three in all (duhh) - Foundation of Food, Arts & Science of Food, and Culinary- Honors. It was a really smart move to take those courses, because I gained so much knowledge about food, so much cultural information, and background info. about food (by the way, if you know of anyone in high school who has an interest in cooking, make a suggestion that they take any culinary courses their school offers- wouldn't want to pass that up).

As every day goes by, my passion for cooking just seems to get stronger and stronger.

Some people may find this odd, but I find cooking to be soothing for me sometimes. It's a time when I can just be myself in the kitchen, to think, be creative, and sing. There's not a time when I'm cooking that the radio is off or my music is not playing. Putting things together, experimenting with different spices, and flavors, using different techniques to come up with something totally new, are part of the fun of cooking. It's a way to express myself, and unleash my creative side and I know it can do the same for you.

Another major benefit I get from cooking is people's reactions. You have no idea how good it makes me feel when I make something new, and people taste it, and love it. I enjoy making others feel good, and one of the ways I do that is through cooking. Cooking is an art, one I'm still in the midst of discovering, and one I intend on mastering someday.

Let me tell you this - I had no idea that I would end up writing a book (e- book if you want to be technical---but eventually it'll be turned into a hard copy). But I think it's pretty important I tell you how it came about. I am in my sophomore year at Johnson & Wales University, studying Culinary Arts (AS), and Food Entrepreneurship (BS). Like most college students, I was worried about money, having a source of income, and most importantly, paying for college. Tuition for college is crazy high, and for most people, it's guaranteed that they will leave college with student loans. My parents and I decided that I would set a goal to graduate college debt free. The only way that would happen is if I apply for as many scholarships as possible, and find a way to have a source of income on summer breaks and while in school. So, I started to try and figure out different ways I could make money- something that would be steady and reliable.
One day, I'm sitting on the living room couch, and my Mom comes by and says to me:

"Hey hon, why don't you try writing an e- book? You could maybe do one on cooking."

After giving it some thought, I decided it was a pretty good idea, we started planning it out. It was a book I could write, on something I LOVE to do, and the best part about it I thought, was that it was not only a way to earn money, but a way to help people, encourage them to be self-sufficient, self-reliant, and to learn a thing or two about food and cooking. This book could focus mainly on kids, college students, and even parents.

I was ecstatic about doing it!

We decided that I would try to get a part-time job, and at the same time put the e- book up for sale; that way I would have two sourCes of income, and I'd be able to rely on myself for the things I want. Then I could also help with college tuition and other expenses. It was truly a win-win situation.

What you've got to try and remember is that, we were a new family. My parents did not have our whole lives to grow our college savings. Their main focus was getting us together as a family, under one roof, and starting off our lives properly: Paying for elementary, middle, and high school, purchasing a new home, the whole 9 yards. Yes, we did have a savings account, but it wasn't nearly as much as it could've been had we started off from day one.

I'm doing ALL that I can to make sure that I can have the experience of being able to graduate, with no loans to pay - (which would mean paying off some loans I had to take last year). As a matter of fact, I just got my first job about a couple of weeks ago, working at a Senior Living home. I went in applying for the position of Dietary Aide, ended up talking to the Dietary Supervisor face to face, and she basically hired me on the spot! Not only that, she told me she wants me to train to be a cook, so I could be one of the chefs. Said she "thinks the experience will be good for me". I went in applying for one job, left with two. I was beyond grateful about what had happened. I couldn't thank God enough.

Back to the point, my hope is that this book, and the ones to come, will help me maintain a steady income throughout college, and that it will help you to feel the same excitement I feel about food, to some degree. My goal is that this book turns out to be a win-win for the both of us. That's the way the mind of an entrepreneur works.

(My parents remind me always that as an entrepreneur I HAVE to be socially conscious and always put helping people before making money – I am a Christian after all, first and foremost)

Since that talk, I've thought of this book as more than just a project, but as a gateway for many more amazing opportunities to come my way. I'm just happy that I am able to share some of what I've learned and hopefully help people in some way. I wrote this book because I enjoy making people happy, I enjoy helping people. I get satisfaction knowing that somewhere out there, in this world of over 7 billion people, someone was able to benefit from what I love doing.

Now, this book addresses a couple of topics like obesity, healthy eating habits, how to save money while in the kitchen, and exercise, even a chapter based on some of Dr. Oz's powerful tips for leading a healthier lifestyle, and his "Power Foods." I've also included the first twenty-one recipes I tried: some I created and some are original recipes I simply made my own by adding my own twist and changing things up. These are recipes I've been working on since my early teens.

There are a couple of things I should explain before we get started. Throughout this book, you will find, next to some of the ingredients, I say "I suggest _____", and there's a link next to it. Those are what you call "affiliate links". By clicking on the link, you will be directed to a page, somewhere on Amazon.com to the product that I am suggesting you use, that will be available for purchase. I did this so you can have the option of purchasing the products I use. And the cool thing about it is, the way affiliates work, if you were to go to that link and decide to buy the product, I get a percentage of that sale. Basically, I'm being paid to "advertise" for them. Pretty cool concept. Another thing you will notice under some recipes is a "C- Note". They're simply notes, or suggestions I may have regarding the recipe.

The "C" is for my name Christian...get it? C? **C**hristian?

In the process of writing this e-book, I've come up with so many new ideas for other books that I plan to release. I'm really looking forward to getting a start on that, as a matter of fact. I really do get joy in being able to help someone through writing about what I love to do.

I want you to enjoy this book, and my biggest hope is that it will bless you in many ways. I thank you in advance for all of your support.

Thanks so much, and God bless you.

Christian Kelly

Safety Tips, Hints & More

   Things happen. Accidents happen. We're human, therefore we are prone to make mistakes. For that reason, safety is a very important topic, especially in the kitchen. In High School, every culinary class I took started with safety and sanitation, and we were tested on it. Why? Because it's important.

   With that being said, I went ahead and put together a list of safety tips, and guidelines for sanitation. Remember... no one likes an unsafe and/or an unclean Chef.

Here are a few suggestions for you to keep in mind in the kitchen...

Regarding Children:

- If your child is making a dish, be sure they are accompanied by an adult.
- Pay close attention when the child is using a knife, or any sharp implement.
- Make sure they receive help when lifting large pots, pans, etc.
- Encourage your kid(s) to use proper measurements.

- Make sure they wash their hands first before they do ANYTHING!
- If applicable, have them tie their hair back before cooking. Wouldn't want to eat a strand of hair, thinking it was pasta, would you?
- Make sure they don't put their hands in their mouths, because not only is it unsanitary, it's unhealthy because if they were just dealing with raw eggs, for example, there's a chance they could catch Salmonella.
- Here are some things kids can do in the kitchen:

  1. Measure out ingredients

  2. Stir/ sift any ingredients

  3. Wash fruits and Veggies

  4. Garnish the food

  5. Peel veggies like cucumbers or potatoes

For everyone else:

- Always be careful and attentive when handling sharp implements no matter how old you are - accidents happen!
- Fire! People assume that just because you fight fire with water, it means that will always be the case. So not true! If you have a grease fire, meaning if your food catches on fire while in the pot, you don't put water on it. You can try and smother it, by attempting to put a lid on the pot (if it's doable), or you can pour Baking Soda on it.
- Fire! Pt 2- Please, always have a fire extinguisher handy, just in case things get out of hand.
- It's always better (and safer) to work with a sharp knife than a dull knife. Why? Because it allows for more precise cuts and it's easier to handle. You don't have to apply so much

pressure, it's swift and easy. Say you cut yourself with a dull knife; Instead of it being a clean cut, a dull knife will drag extra flesh making it even more painful and worse than a wound with a sharp knife. Make sure your knives are sharp, and sharpen them as needed.

- When cutting poultry, raw meat, fish, or anything of that sort, use a separate cutting board from what you would normally use to cut vegetables and fruit and so on. If you don't have two cutting boards, use the reverse side – but MAKE SURE you scrub it with bleach and hot soapy water.

- This is common sense, but people still don't do it - when cooking, make sure the handles of the pot are not sticking out, that way there will be less chance of an accident happening.

- Before you start preparing your meal, it's sensible to get everything out, so that you won't have to worry about going back and forth from the stove to the cupboards, and you won't have to rush to get out the next ingredient, and accidentally pick up cinnamon, thinking it's chili powder (my Mom did that one time). It saves time, trust me. Up at school, we call that Mise En Place - (its French meaning you have everything out and ready to go).

- Over the years, I've realized that it's best to keep some sort of small container dedicated to garbage so that your area won't be so dirty. Chefs do it all the time.

- Speaking of a dirty area, I find it difficult to work when my area is cluttered with junk - that's why I advise you to clean up as you go along; it'll make life much easier.

- ALWAYS wash fruits and vegetables, even if they came prepackaged.

- Here are some knives that are crucial to have when in the kitchen

- Chef's knife
- Paring knife
- Boning knife
- Bread knife

You will use these knives the most, so it's best to have them handy.

- Back to the topic of boards - if you are deciding which type of cutting board is best to use, here's the answer: Wooden cutting boards are the best to use because they don't dull your knives down anywhere near as fast as plastic ones do. I'm not saying it's bad to use plastic boards, I'm saying it's better to use wooden.

- When handling hot pot handles, always use pot holders, or oven mitts, or a kitchen towel - but make sure the kitchen towel doesn't get anywhere near the flame, or it'll be the last time you see it.

- Here's one you probably know about since you were a little kid - never, ever, EVER use an electrical appliance with wet hands - unless you want a new hair-do.

- Temperature is important! If there's one thing that the Chefs at school stress, it's making sure that your finished product (meaning when the food is fully cooked and ready to be served), is at its correct temp.

Ground Meat: 160°F

Fresh Beef, Veal, Lamb: 145°F

Poultry: 165°F

Pork & Ham: 145°F

Seafood: 145°F

- Throughout the recipes, you may come across abbreviations you may not understand, so here is a quick legend of what they mean

  T= Tablespoon

  t= teaspoon

  c= cup

  pck= pack

  lrg= large

- I'm sure you are well aware of the concept of the food pyramid, correct? Well, forget about it, completely disregard it! I was watching an episode of Dr. Oz, and he had guest speaker Dr. Joel Furhrman who was discussing his version of the food pyramid is the key to a healthy lifestyle.

Instead of this:

It should be this:

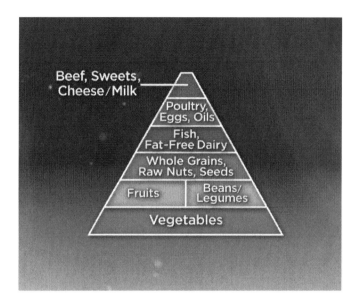

(photo credit of doctoroz.com)

Notice that Dr. Fuhrman's pyramid starts with Vegetables and fruits & beans/ legumes as the base. He believes that these foods, which are high in micro- nutrients are most important to consume, and he believes that these foods "contain vitamins and minerals that are essential to helping the body repair itself, they also have immune-boosting phytochemicals."

Must-Haves

It can be hard to do a good job, when you don't have the right tools. The same goes for cooking. You can't really make a dish turn out as best as it could without the proper tools. Below is a list of what every kitchen should have. It may seem like a lot, but it's really not. They will come in handy one time or another. Go through the list, then take a quick inventory of your kitchen to see what you do and don't have.

I recommend that you buy the things you don't have whenever you get the chance.

Pots/ pans/ electrical

- 12" fry pan
- 3 qt non-stick saucepot
- 12" skillet with lid
- 8 qt Dutch Oven
- 16 qt stock pot (if you make large quantities of soup and/ or stews)
- 10" cast iron skillet
- 14" Wok
- 12" sauté pan
- Muffin pan
- Porcelain/ ceramic casserole dishes
- Food processor
- Blender
- Electric mixer
- Cake pans
- Roasting pan

practice them often. My hope is that they work for you, and you will at least give them a try, and if you like them, stick to them. You seriously will be amazed at the changes over time.

Here are some tips for healthy eating habits:

- Try to incorporate at least two types of fruit and vegetables into your diet, daily.

- When you get ready to use any fruit or vegetable, WASH IT. No matter how clean or spotless it looks, you must wash it. You have no idea the amount of pesticides that may have been used on it. (A popular solution is 3 parts water, 1 part vinegar.)

- Have a copy of the *New* Food Pyramid posted somewhere in your kitchen so that you can be reminded of what to eat, and what to stay away from (*ChooseMyPlate.gov* is an excellent site to visit- it allows you to calculate the nutritional value of any meal, lets you create daily food plans, tells you how much of each food group you should consume- things of that nature).

- It is much healthier to consume 6 meals per day - I don't mean six *dinner* meals, I mean light meals. The only meals that should be somewhat 'heavy' are breakfast, lunch, and dinner. Besides these, try to fill in the rest of the six meals with some healthy snacks.

- It's best to have the heavier meal earlier in the day – making dinner light.

- Eat heavier meals earlier in the day if possible. No heavy meals within 3 hours of bedtime.

- *Don't eat with your eyes, eat with your mind!* Better yet, wait for your *brain* to send the message that you're full. Just because there may be a variety of things for you to choose from at any given meal time doesn't mean you have to have some of everything; it just means you have to pick and choose, OR just have a tiny bit of everything. Eating with your eyes is what causes your weight to spike up, and causes you to overeat. This is actually what I do at buffets, on cruises and so forth. I eat a very little bit of EVERYTHING I want to try. As long as my plate is not too full, I'm good.

- Try to have salad with dinner and even lunch. Not only is it healthy, and ensures that you get in some vegetables into your diet; it can add flavor and appearance to your dish, even color. Salad isn't always boring; it just depends on how you make it. Spicing it up with some fruit, maybe some nuts (walnuts and almonds are the best, I think), or croutons makes it taste way better. Salad is an easy side dish you could have your children help with to get them accustomed to cutting, and handling a knife

- How often do you drink water? When you're thirsty, and there's no soda or juice in the cupboard or fridge? I SINCERELY hope that's not the case. You should consume at *least* 8 glasses of water per day. Whenever you feel thirsty, treat yourself to some water instead of reaching for that soda or juice. Water is the **best** thirst quencher, not Gatorade or Pepsi. Also, try having water with your meals. If you really don't want to compromise your juice, soda, or whatever it is you usually drink, alternate the days with water, if you think that would be helpful. For example, Monday, you would have what you normally have, but come Tuesday, it's back to water and so on.

- When you usually eat dinner, where do you eat? In front the TV? The kitchen table? Outside, maybe? If you know you have a habit of eating in front of the TV, you have got to try and put an end to that. Believe it or not, eating in front of the TV actually causes you to eat faster, which makes you want seconds, thirds, even fourths! You're not focused on your food, and are not actually tasting, and enjoying it. Instead, your mind is focused on what you're watching. Try sitting at the table with the kids or your parents or spouse, and talk. Or, if by yourself, try reading a book. See if you notice the difference compared to when you were in front the TV. Trust me, you won't regret breaking that habit.

- *Read. Be aware!* Look at what is going into your body by reading the food labels of what you buy. Familiarize yourself with things you should stay away from, and foods you should get more accustomed to eating.

- *Fat you don't need-* when you cook with chicken, how often do you bother to remove the skin? Sometimes? All the time? Never? Sometimes leaving the skin on can be good in terms of giving flavor, but not all the time. Removing the skin is an excellent step to taking away some of that unnecessary fat. I do it just about all the time.

- *Super sweet sugar.* When you sweeten your tea, or your cereal or your cookies, or cakes, or whatever else you use sugar for, what kind of sugar do you use? And how much? Consider using substitutes like Agave, Maple Syrup, or Raw sugar, (a healthier alternative). I learned from a friend at school that processed sugar actually contains **Aspartame** which (according to *WebMD)* has actually been linked to Cancer, Diabetes, Psychological Disorders, Birth Defects, Vision Problems, and even Brain Damage & Seizures.

   So, like I stated before, try incorporating these tips, attempt to make them a habit, and see for yourself the differences that will occur.

Recipes:

In this chapter, you'll find my first 21 recipes. Like I said earlier, some of them are spinoffs of traditional recipes, but I customized them, and they still came out amazing. There are dishes for breakfast, lunch, dinner, and desserts. Now, the good thing about these recipes is that for the most part, they're pretty simple, and easy to follow. They're inexpensive, and most of them are really quick to make. You can use leftovers to make some of them (which can be really convenient and cost effective).

I'll always remember these dishes as my "First 21". The first 21 recipes I tried when my passion for cooking started to manifest. The first recipe I actually tried was the Shrimp with Angel Hair Pasta. That was a throwback. The recipes that I created will be labeled "O" signifying it was an original. Some of them I first tried out when I was about 14 years old. My hope is that you will enjoy them as much as I did.

Breakfast

Oatmeal with fruit topping- "O"

(Best way to start your day!)

Cook/prep time- 20 min

What you need:

- Uncooked Oats (I suggest Quaker http://amzn.to/12MrRrP)
- Strawberries
- Blueberries
- Raisins
- Chopped walnuts
- Grapes
- Bananas (optional)
- 1 T cinnamon
- ½ t Nutmeg
- Salt to taste

- **100 % Agave Nectar or Maple- syrup**
- **Your favorite milk**

What to do:

Cook oats according to directions - but, before the water comes to a boil, add the cinnamon, nutmeg and salt.

Meanwhile, slice all your fruits to bite size pieces; on a plate, have all your berries, raisins, walnuts, bananas, and grapes ready to go. Once the oatmeal is done, serve it out in a bowl, add as much milk as you'd like, along with the fruits and nuts.

Lightly drizzle some Agave or Maple Syrup over the oatmeal, if needed. This will serve as your sweetener.

C- Note

One thing I started using lately is Almond Milk. If you're worried about how much sugar you consume, try using Almond milk. Sweetened Almond Milk can be used as a substitute for Agave or Maple Syrup.

Banapes (Banana Crepes)- "O"

Fast & Easy!

Cook/prep time- 15 min

What you need:

- **Pancake Mix (I suggest Aunt Jemima http://amzn.to/1eh7yTn)**
- **2 ripe bananas**
- **Extra Virgin Olive Oil**
- **Cinnamon- to taste**
- **Nutmeg- to taste**
- **Natural Strawberry Jam (I suggest Smuckers http://amzn.to/1pFRPUo)**

What to do:

Prepare the pancake mix as directed. Before you start to cook them, mash up the bananas really well, and add them to the mix (the mix should be slightly lumpy by now).

Lightly coat the bottom of the pan with olive oil. Start to cook the crepes by pouring about 5 tablespoons of the mix into the pan. If you put too much, it'll be too thick.

Quickly cover the entire pan with the mix by shaking it around until it spreads entirely. Don't use a spoon or anything else to do this. Let it cook for a few minutes on **medium-low** heat, until bubbles start to form at the top.

Once you lift the crepe up (it should be thin), flip it, and cook the other side. Continue the process until the mix is finished.

Spread some strawberry jam on the inside of crepe, lightly sprinkle a little Cinnamon and Nutmeg (optional) over the jam, and roll it up from one end to the other.

Serve with turkey bacon, and maybe some eggs, and enjoy.

Scrambled Omelet- "O"

Cook/prep time- 10 min

What you need:

- **2 large eggs**
- **¼ small onion diced**
- **¼ small green pepper diced**
- **½ small tomato diced**
- **1 scallion diced**
- **2 slices turkey bacon diced (I used Oscar Meyer)**
- **Shredded cheddar cheese or Pepper Jack Cheese**
- **¼ t salt**
- **½ t black pepper**

- **2 T milk or water**
- **1 T onion powder (optional)**
- **3 t <u>un</u>salted butter**

What to do:

Melt the butter in a pan over medium heat. Once hot enough add the onion, pepper, scallion, tomato, and bacon. Cook on medium heat for 2 to 3 minutes.

Crack the eggs and beat them. Add the salt, black pepper, onion powder, and milk/ water.

Pour the egg mixture over the bacon and vegetables in the pan, and turn the heat to medium low. Push the eggs from side to side, forming "mountains" so that there can be more room for it to cook. Once it's solid, thoroughly fold the eggs over and over again so that the veggies can get mixed into the eggs. It'll be done once you see no more liquid and soft "peaks" have formed.

Sprinkle the shredded cheese over the eggs, turn off the heat, and let it sit about a minute so it can melt. Serve with turkey bacon, lightly buttered whole wheat bread and your favorite juice.

Ackee and Salt Fish

This is a famous Jamaican recipe, made with bacalao (salt fish), veggies, and Ackee. Originally from West Africa, Ackee is a Jamaican fruit that grows on Ackee trees, and it bears a bright red fruit. The first time my dad made it, I could have sworn it was scrambled eggs, no lie! Ackee **looks** just like that, but **tastes** excellent.

Cook/prep time- 45 min

What You need:

- 1 large yellow onion (½ sliced, ½ diced)`
- 1 medium tomato- chopped`
- 3 stalks of green onion (scallion)- chopped
- 1 bag of salt fish
- 1 can of Ackee (I suggest http://amzn.to/19CqRsJ)
- ½ green pepper- sliced
- ½ red pepper- sliced
- ½ yellow pepper- sliced
- 3 sprig of thyme

- **Onion Powder- to taste**
- **2 cloves garlic**
- **Extra virgin olive oil**
- **¼ t black pepper**
- **Large tomato- chopped**

What to do:

You want to start by un-salting the fish. You can do this by putting it in a pot of water and let it come to a boil. Dump that water out, refill the pot, and bring to a boil again. This will help thoroughly remove most of the salt. Taste a piece of the fish to see if it's still too salty. If it is, bring to a boil one more time. Finally, run some cold water over the fish, and pat it dry.

Break the fish up, but not to the point that you can't pick it up by fork. *The bigger the pieces, the more flavor it will add and the more you will be able to taste it in the dish*

In a medium skillet, heat 3 tablespoons of the olive oil and once it's hot enough, add the **diced** onion and garlic and sauté for a minute.

Add the scallion, peppers, and the sliced onions. Sauté for about 3 minutes on medium heat. Then put in the fish and cook for another 5 minutes, stirring occasionally on a medium heat. Now throw in the tomato and mix thoroughly, and cook for another 5 minutes.

Before adding the Ackee, open the can and drain it to get almost all the liquid out. Now add it in, along with the season salt. Mix thoroughly and let it cook for about 5 minutes.

Serve with boiled OR fried plantain and or lightly toasted and lightly buttered Potato Bread.

Enjoy!

C- Note

Ackee isn't a product you'd find in your typical supermarket. You'll most likely have to check a local farmers or a supermarket market to see if they have it.

Lunch

Personal Chicken Salad- "O"

Easy!

Not only is this easy and quick to make, but it tastes amazing.

Cook/prep time- 15 min

What you need:

- **Romaine and Iceberg Lettuce – equal parts (I use Foxy brand)**
- **1 tomato**
- **½ green pepper- julienned (sliced into strips)**
- **½ cucumber**
- **½ apple- chopped**
- **6 strawberries**
- **¼ c raisins**
- **Chopped walnuts**
- **½ red pepper- sliced**

- **Asian Toasted Sesame Dressing (I suggest Kraft http://amzn.to/1cwzrc1)**
- **Rotisserie Chicken (Try Costco if it's available)**

What to do:

Cut the chicken into sizable strips.

Chop half of the Iceberg lettuce and Romaine lettuce and put into a bowl. Set aside.

Peel and chop the apple. Slice the strawberries, and combine with the lettuce. Add the peppers too.

Chop the tomato. Peel the cucumber and slice it so that you get large ⅛" coins, and add that to the lettuce. Combine the chicken with the lettuce mixture, and top with the raisins and walnuts.

Serve out in bowls, and drizzle the Asian dressing over the salad. Enjoy!

Saucy sausage n' Pasta-   "O"

This is a good dish for kids to make

Cook/prep time- 30 min

What you need:

- ¾ link Turkey Kielbasa (I use Hillshire Farms)
- ½ green pepper- sliced
- ½ large onion- sliced
- ½ large tomato- sliced
- 4 T ketchup
- Box elbow pasta (I suggest Barilla http://amzn.to/WD0Tl0)
- ½ T chili powder
- ½ T season salt

- ¾ cup tomato sauce
- Worcestershire Sauce (I suggest Lea & Perrins http://amzn.to/12Mrhuc)
- Extra Virgin Olive Oil
- Hot sauce (optional)

What to do:

Cook pasta according to directions.

Coat the pan with olive oil on medium heat. Meanwhile, slice the Kielbasa in little "coins" and set aside. Once the oil is ready, cook the Kielbasa, onions, and peppers for 8 minutes on medium heat, stirring occasionally.

Lower the heat and add the tomatoes, season salt, and chili powder. Mix thoroughly and cook for another 2 minutes. Don't allow it to get too mushy.

Now add the ketchup, and Worcestershire sauce, and tomato sauce, and simmer for a few more minutes. Add the water (so that it gets a little saucy) and mix. Turn off the heat.

Serve over the pasta, and have it with Tea-monade (found in the "Side Dishes")

C- Note

The very first time I made this, I used hot dogs because I didn't have sausage at the time. Hot dogs work just as well if you don't have sausage, and it tastes great.

Festive Fried Rice- "O"

Fast!

Cook/prep time- 25 min

What you need:

- Cooked brown rice
- ½ large yellow onion
- 2 cloves garlic- diced
- 1 can or 1 pack frozen mixed vegetables
- 2 stalks of scallions
- Cooked chicken (preferably rotisserie)- chopped
- Season salt (to taste)

- **2 T Chili powder**
- **1 T sesame oil**
- **4 T Extra Virgin Olive Oil**

What to do:

Dice the onion, scallion, and garlic.

Using a wok, heat the olive oil, and add the sesame oil to it.

* Make sure to watch the pot, because oil tends to get hot really fast when heated in a wok.

Add the onion, scallion, and garlic to the oil and cook for about a 15 sec. Do NOT let the garlic burn!

Add the rice, and push it to one side of the wok. On the other side, add the chicken. The wok should be divided with the rice on one side and chicken on the other to allow both to cook separately. Now mix thoroughly, and continue to cook for about 10 minutes, mixing occasionally as to not let the food burn.

In the meantime, drain all the liquid from the mixed vegetables (if you're using canned veggies), and add it to the rice, along with the season salt and chili powder. Mix, then let it cook for another 5 minutes

Serve hot.

C- Note

It's traditional to add bits of fried egg in Fried Rice, hence you can see I added it in my recipe. But it is optional, not everyone does it.

Homemade Hamburger Helper- "O"

Cook/prep time- 30 min

What you need:

- Extra virgin olive oil
- 3 uncooked hamburger patties- cut into cubes
- 1 green pepper (1/2 diced, ½ sliced)
- 1 medium yellow onion (1/2 diced, ½ sliced)
- ½ red pepper- diced
- 1 box of pasta elbows
- 2 T hamburger seasonings (I suggest McCormick http://amzn.to/19Cr3lf)
- 1 T black pepper
- 3 scallions- chopped
- 1 can sweet peas
- 1 large tomato- diced
- ¼ c shredded cheddar cheese

What to do:

Cook the pasta according to directions.

Get a large skillet, and heat oil in it. Add the cubed patties. Cook for 10 minutes.

Now add in the chopped scallions, all the onions, and half the green peppers, and all the red pepper. Mix together and cook for 5 minutes stirring occasionally.

Add the hamburger seasoning then the tomato, and peas and the rest of the peppers. Stir, and then add the black pepper. Cook for another 5 minutes, stirring constantly.

Drain the pasta and pour it back into the pot that it cooked in. Put the cooked burger and veggies in the pot with the pasta, and mix thoroughly. Sprinkle the cheese over it and mix.

Serve hot and ENJOY!!

Dinner

Shrimp with Angel Hair Pasta- "O"

In an attempt to make shrimp scampi, I ended up producing a different product. It's similar, and tastes great. Thank God for mistakes!!

Cook/prep time- 30 min

What you need:

- **1 bag cooked shrimp**
- **2 scallions- chopped**
- **1 medium yellow onion- diced**
- **Sun dried tomatoes- chopped**
- **1 Tomato- diced**
- **½ large green pepper- diced**

- ½ large red pepper cut into- diced
- Extra virgin olive oil
- 1 T butter (unsalted)
- 1 box whole grain angel hair pasta
- Black pepper
- 1 packet Sazon seasoning (I suggest Goya http://amzn.to/1cwyzUA)
- 2 T Worcestershire sauce (I suggest Lea & Perrins http://amzn.to/12Mrhuc)
- ¼ t Chili powder

What to do:

Cook pasta according to directions.

In a medium skillet, heat 3 T of the oil and the 1 T of butter. Once that's hot enough, add the scallions, onion, sun dried tomatoes, green pepper, and the red pepper. Sauté for about 5 minutes on medium heat until translucent, or, its clear.

Add the shrimp, and cook for about 5 minutes on medium high heat, stirring a couple of times. Add 2 teaspoons of black pepper, half of the Sazon Goya, chili powder, and the Worcestershire sauce.

Throw in the chopped tomato. Stir thoroughly, and remove from heat.

Garnish with chopped cilantro on top, serve over a bed of pasta, pour yourself a glass of Tea-monade, and ENJOY!!

Turkey Chili Joes- "O"

Cook time- 30 min

What you need:

- 1 large onion
- 1 large green pepper
- 2 cloves garlic- diced
- 2 T Goya Season Salt
- 2 T chili powder
- 2 t black pepper
- 1 t salt
- 1 can red kidney beans (optional)
- Ketchup
- Tomato sauce

- ½ fresh tomato- chopped
- ½ canned diced tomato
- 1 pack ground turkey meat
- Whole Wheat hamburger buns
- Extra Virgin Olive Oil

What to do:

Dice the garlic, half of the onion, and the entire green pepper, and combine with the turkey meat. Add to that the chili powder, season salt, black pepper, and salt; combine thoroughly with your hands.

In a large sauce pan, heat enough olive oil to coat the bottom, plus about a tablespoon more. After a minute, add the diced garlic and chopped onion to the pot. Sauté for one minute. Add the turkey meat, and cook, stirring occasionally for 10 minutes, or until no longer pink.

Add the ketchup, both fresh and canned tomatoes, tomato sauce, and red beans. Mix thoroughly and simmer for 10 minutes. Season with a bit more salt if needed.

Toast the hamburger buns, and then top them with chili. Before you sit down to eat, make sure you have A LOT of napkins, and enjoy!

Chicken Parm with homemade tomato sauce

Cook/prep time- 1 hr

What you need:

- 1 box whole wheat spaghetti (I use Barilla)
- 2 eggs + 1 T milk
- Italian style bread crumbs (I suggest Progresso http://amzn.to/13terQ0)
- ½ c grated Mozzarella cheese
- 2 T garlic powder or salt
- 2 t salt
- 2 T onion powder
- 2 T season salt (Adobo)
- 2 T Italian Seasoning (I use McCormick)
- Extra Virgin Olive Oil
- 4 boneless skinless chicken breast

For the Sauce

- **2 large tomatoes chopped**
- **5 T ketchup**
- **2 T Worcestershire Sauce**
- **¼ c tomato sauce**
- **1 T sugar**
- **1 T dried crushed Basil**
- **1 t Italian Seasoning**

What to do:

Preheat oven to 350° F

Cook the pasta according to directions

Clean the chicken with vinegar, and pat dry. Season with garlic powder, salt, onion powder, and season salt.

In one bowl, put the bread crumbs and in another the eggs and milk.

Coat the bottom of a large saucepan with olive oil plus a little more. Start the process by dipping the chicken in the egg mixture then coat with bread crumbs. Lay in the pan and cook for 10 minutes. Flip to make sure both sides are browned. Once they're all done, lay them in a baking dish.

For the sauce, in a blender, put the diced tomato with ketchup, Worcestershire sauce and tomato sauce, and pulse for 30 seconds. Now add the crushed basil and Italian Seasoning. Pulse for another 30 seconds. (To make it thicker, add more tomato sauce or ketchup until it as thick as you'd like). Set aside.

Sprinkle the mozzarella over all of chicken. Then add enough sauce to cover the chicken, NOT drown it. Bake for 20 minutes until the chicken has reached an internal temp of 165°F.

Serve over spaghetti, but make sure you add the tomato sauce to it, and enjoy!

Finger Lickin' Stew Chicken- "O"

(photo cred to cronuspersonaltraining.com)

Cook time- 45 min

What you need:

- **2 packs of chicken - 1 drumsticks, 1 thighs**
- **1 T Salt**
- **2 T Garlic powder**
- **1 t Turmeric**
- **2 T Chili powder**
- **2 t Paprika**
- **2 t Cayenne pepper**
- **1 T Black pepper**
- **3 T Goya seasoning**

- **2 lrg yellow onions**
- **1 lrg tomato**
- **2 cloves garlic**
- **2 stalks scallion**
- **½ green pepper**
- **½ red pepper**
- **Coconut Milk (I suggest Grace http://amzn.to/14oGoeA)**
- **½ chicken bouillon cube**
- **¼ c Ketchup**
- **½ c Caribbean Jerk Marinade**
- **1 T Honey**
- **½ c Barbecue sauce**
- **Vinegar**
- **Canned Sweet corn**
- **Canned String beans**

What to do:

Remove all the skin from the chicken. Discard. Place the chicken in a large bowl and clean it with vinegar. Drain it, and then rinse with cold water. Pat dry.

Season with the first eight ingredients. Toss the chicken so that all pieces are coated evenly. Now add about ¼ of a cup of ketchup, the honey, ¼ cup of the barbecue sauce, and ½ cup of the marinade. Toss again so that all pieces are covered. Now dice half of one of the onions, and chop one of the stalks of scallion and sprinkle over the chicken, and let it sit.

Dice the garlic, the other half of the onion, and scallion. Get a large pot and generously coat the bottom of it with olive oil, and heat it. While the oil is getting hot, grate the bouillon cube until it's powdery. By this time, the oil should be hot enough. Throw in the garlic, onion, scallion, and the bullion. Reduce the heat to medium, and cook for a minute.

Now get your chicken and one by one lay then in the bottom of the pot, fitting as many pieces as you can before you start to lay them on top of each other. Save any liquid from the bowl for later. Let it cook until all the pieces have had the chance to brown on each side. Once they're all browned, cover the pot and let it simmer for 20 minutes on medium high heat, periodically checking the pot to see that the chicken isn't sticking.

Slice the rest of the onion, and the peppers, and chop the tomatoes, and set them aside. Take whatever liquid that was left over from the bowl with the chicken and pour that into the pot. Add the onions and peppers and tomatoes, and let it sit again for about 10 minutes on medium heat.

Pour about half of the can of coconut milk into the pot and stir. Let it simmer for 5 minutes, and then put in the string beans and corn. Simmer for 5 minutes one last time. Make sure you now have a semi thick, flavorful, gravy. Taste it to make sure it's good. If more seasoning is needed, I suggest adding some season salt, but not a lot. Lawry's is fine.

Serve over some steamed rice and some salad to accompany the meal, and enjoy!

Stew Fish with Mango- Pineapple Salsa- "O"

Cook/prep time- 45 min

What you need:

- 1 pack frozen Tilapia- thawed
- ½ lrg green pepper- sliced to strips
- ½ lrg red pepper- sliced to strips
- 1 lrg red onion- ½ chopped ½ sliced
- 2 cloves garlic- diced
- 2 scallion stalks- chopped
- 1 large tomato- diced
- 2 T Season salt (I use Adobo http://amzn.to/16ptWct)
- Black pepper
- Vinegar
- Extra virgin olive oil
- 4 sprigs thyme

For the Salsa

- ¼ c medium pineapple
- 1 mango
- ½ green pepper
- ½ small red onion- diced
- 1 medium tomato- chopped
- Hot sauce
- ½ cup Mango- peach salsa (I *highly* recommend Santa Barbara)
- Cinnamon

What to do:

Clean the tilapia with vinegar, then rinse with cold water and pat dry. Season the fish with the season salt, covering all pieces, and then lightly sprinkle black pepper on top of that. Throw in the thyme and mix thoroughly, but handle the fish gently because Tilapia tends to be very fragile. Set aside.

In a large skillet, heat the olive oil and sauté the chopped red onion, the garlic, half the green & red pepper, and the entire scallion, for a minute.

Now carefully lay the fish on top the vegetables and let that cook, covered on a medium heat for 10 minutes, flipping twice so that it cooks through and through.

In the meantime, finely chop the pineapple, mango, green pepper, and tomato, but make sure it isn't diced. ONLY dice the onion. Get a small saucepan and heat 1 T of olive oil. Once it's good and hot, toss in the pepper, onion and tomato. Cook it on a medium heat for about 5 minutes then add the pineapple and mango.

Now add in a tablespoon of hot sauce (I used Goya), and 1 cup of the mango peach salsa. Cook for another 5 minutes, but watch it to make sure it doesn't get too soggy. Now, add in ½ teaspoon cinnamon, give it a good mix and turn off the heat.

Back to the fish, flip the pieces over, and get some of the juices from the bottom of the pan and pour it on top of the fish, giving it a chance to soak up the flavor. Add the rest of the onions, the peppers, and put in the tomato. Cover again and let it sit for about 2-3 minutes, or until done.

Serve this dish with a nice rice pilaf, top the fish with the mango-pineapple salsa (or put it on the side), and some salad.

Hope you fall in love with it. I did!

Ginger Curry Chicken - "O"

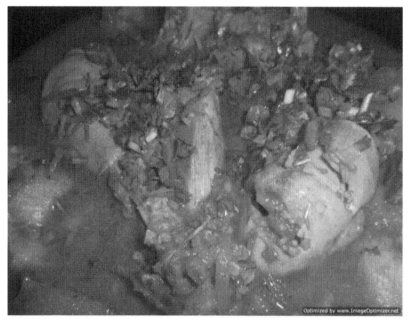

Cook/prep time- 70 min

What you need:

- ¼ of a root of ginger- finely grated
- 2 packs of chicken (1 pack drumsticks, 1 pack thighs)
- 5 T Curry powder- (for as long as I've been doing curry, I ALWAYS try to use Blue Mountain. It's a really good brand http://amzn.to/14NIc9S)
- 1 t Turmeric
- 1 T Salt
- 1 T Black pepper
- ½ c seafood stock
- 3 stalks scallion- chopped
- 1 lrg onion- chopped
- 1 can Sweet corn

- 1 can String beans
- 1 large tomato
- 1 can Coconut milk
- Thyme- 2 sprigs
- Vinegar
- 3 cloves garlic- minced
- ½ green pepper- chopped
- ½ red pepper- chopped
- Extra Virgin Olive Oil

What to do:

Wash the chicken with the vinegar, and rinse with cold water. Pat dry and place in a large bowl. Season with the salt, black pepper, 5 tablespoons of the curry powder, and the Turmeric. Throw in the 2 sprigs of thyme and toss it so that all pieces of chicken are evenly coated, and let it sit for a minimum of 20 minutes.

In a large pot, generously coat the bottom with olive oil and let it sit about a minute until it gets hot enough. Now put in the garlic, the ginger, onion, and sprinkle 1 tablespoon of curry powder and cook for 30 seconds stirring constantly so the garlic doesn't burn.

Lay the chicken in the pot, fitting as many possible on the bottom. Let those pieces get a chance to brown on each side, before taking them out. Remove them, set aside, and put in the rest of the chicken and do the same thing (you only need to do this if the pot isn't big enough to fit all in at once)

After all the pieces are browned, put them all in the pot, and add another 3 T of curry powder, and mix well. Pour in ½ cup of seafood stock and let it simmer on a medium low heat for 20 minutes. Then add the rest of the onions, the corn, string beans, and the tomato.

Pour in about ½ of the can of coconut milk, and let it cook. After 15 minutes, check to see the inside is no longer pink, and the chicken has reached an internal temp of 165. If not, allow it to cook longer.

Accompany this dish with rice and salad, and enjoy.

Dessert

Smoo- Pops- "O"

Quick & Easy!

Cook/prep time- 10 min

What you need:

- **2 bananas- chopped**
- **1 cup strawberries- hulled (remove stems) and chopped**
- **Generous ¾ cup plain yogurt**
- **Agave Nectar**
- **Maple Syrup**
- **Ice pop molds**
- **Popsicle sticks**

What to do:

In a blender place the bananas, strawberries and the yogurt, and blend until smooth. Then add 1 T of Agave and 2 T of maple syrup, and blend for a couple more seconds.

Pour the smoothie into the ice pop molds and freeze. After about 30 minutes, place the Popsicle sticks on the mold so that they stand up straight, and place it in the freezer again, until fully frozen.

Remove from the freezer and enjoy as a healthy snack, or for dessert.

Strawberry- Cinnamon Shortcakes w/ Vanilla Cream- "O"

Cook/prep time- 20 min

What you need:

- **Pillsbury Grand's Biscuits**
- **Fresh strawberries- hulled**
- **Strawberry preserves (Jam- I suggest Smuckers http:// amzn.to/16pttH9)**
- **Cinnamon**
- **Nutmeg**
- **3 T Maple Syrup**

For the Cream:

- **1 cup COLD Heavy Whipping Cream**

- **1 t Vanilla Extract**
- **2 T granulated sugar**

What to do:

Slice the strawberries, and place them in a small bowl. Combine the Strawberry preserves, ¼ t cinnamon, ⅛ t of nutmeg, and the syrup. Mix well and set it in the fridge for half hour. Let it obtain a thick consistency.

Cook the biscuits according to package, set aside and keep warm.

In a bowl, whisk the heavy cream with broad strokes, trying to incorporate as much air as you can. Rotate directions every so often. Whisk until the cream starts to thicken. Stop, add in the vanilla and sugar, and whisk again until soft peaks start to form. Make sure the cream is stiff enough to "stand up", but not as thick as butter. You DO NOT want that. Set aside.

Gather your biscuits and cut them in half. On the bottom half, spoon out some of the strawberry mixture, then top it with the whipped cream. Dust a little bit of cinnamon on top the cream, and place the top on.

Enjoy, they taste amazing!

C- Note

- Make sure not to over-beat the cream because it could become lumpy, or too thick, and that would ruin it.
- For best results, before you start, make sure the bowl and whisk you use are ice cold. That might mean placing them in the freezer before use.

Side Dishes

Basic- Every day- Salad- "O"

Easy!

This is what my family and I have, just about every time we cook. It adds color to the dish, and it's healthy. We usually use salad dressing, but have some self- control when you use it, and don't flood the salad; it just defeats the whole purpose.

Cook/prep time- 10 min

What you need:

- **Romaine lettuce**
- **Cucumbers**
- **Ripe Vine Tomatoes**
- **Green pepper**

- **Red pepper**

What to do:

Wash & chop & dry the lettuce; place it in a salad bowl.

Peel the cucumber, and chop into large coins with ⅛" thickness. If you want, leave the skin on, and just chop it. Place it in the bowl with the lettuce.

Slice the green and red pepper into ½" long strips and place in the bowl. Chop the tomatoes and place them in the bowl too.

Thoroughly mix the salad together.

C- Note

- For this recipe, I don't use exact measurements because it all depends on how many people you are serving. I just use my judgment whenever I make salad.

- Usually, when I make my salad, I always add other ingredients like shredded carrots, raisins, chopped walnuts, craisins, mandarins, chopped apples. All of these add crunch, flavor, and texture to the salad.

Beans- Cubed (Basic Black Beans)- "O"

Quick & Easy!

Such a simple name for such a simple recipe. This too makes an excellent side dish.

Cook/prep time- 15 min

What you need:

- **1 can Black Beans or Red Kidney Beans (I suggest Goya- http://amzn.to/1npM6Dy)**
- **1 small red onion- chopped**
- **2 cloves garlic- minced**
- **½ green pepper- chopped**
- **1 small tomato- chopped**
- **1 stalk scallion- chopped**
- **Extra Virgin Olive Oil**
- **Salt**
- **Hot sauce**

What to do:

In a large sauce pan, heat 3 tablespoons of olive oil

Add the garlic, onion, and scallion to the oil and cook for a minute. Lower the heat a little and add the beans. Simmer on a medium heat for 10 minutes.

Now add the green pepper, tomato, and hot sauce to taste. Season with season salt. Mix well.
Garnish with chopped Cilantro. Enjoy.

Sautéed Spinach

This makes an excellent healthy side dish to almost any meal. It's quick and easy.

Cook/prep time- 20 min

What you need:

- **2 packs of fresh spinach**
- **2 cloves garlic**
- **1 small red onion**
- **½ lemon**
- **½ T unsalted butter**
- **Extra Virgin Olive Oil**
- **Salt**
- **Chili Powder**

What to do:

Place the spinach in a strainer and wash with cold water to remove any excess dirt that may still be on it. Dry it and set aside.

Mince the garlic and finely chop the onion. In a 12" skillet, heat 4 tablespoons of olive oil, and the butter. Once it's hot enough, add the garlic and onion, and cook for a minute. Reduce the heat a little before the garlic starts to burn.

Add the spinach to the pot, put a lid on it, and let it sit until the spinach starts to wilt. Stir periodically so that the spinach doesn't stick.

After about 5 minutes, squeeze the lemon over the spinach, sprinkle 2 tablespoons of chili powder over it and mix. After another 5 minutes, turn off the heat and **lightly** sprinkle salt over all the spinach.

C- Note

If you'd like, sprinkle some hot sauce over the spinach. This adds a little flavor. I do it from time to time, and it tastes really good.

I saw on Dr. Oz that it's really good to use Coconut oil, and it's healthy. So if you prefer, you can substitute that for the olive oil, and it'll still taste good.

Tea-monade –"O"

After craving some lemonade for a while, I decided to experiment with what I had at home. I had everything; the lemons, the water… but not the SUGAR! That's when I asked the big bad wolf to go and get some for me!!! Get it?!?! Big bad wolf, 3 little pigs…..maybe that was a little corny …but anyway, I got what I think is a pretty good outcome.

What you need:

- **1 lemon**
- **1 cup water (room temp)**
- **3 T maple syrup**
- **Ice**
- **Tea bag (fruit or herbal flavor of your choice)**

What to do:

Juice the lemon with a juicer (electric or manual…I prefer the manual...gives you a quick work out). Put the juice in a cup and add water. Stir, and see how it tastes. If it's too tart, add more water. Make sure you don't water it down though. Now put in the tea bag (it can be any flavor: Raspberry Zinger, Cherry Zinger, Mint, Peppermint, anything). Let it sit for 5-10 minutes. Now add the maple syrup. Stir well, and add ice if you'd like. Enjoy

C- Note

Maple syrup may sound weird, but don't judge until you've tried it. It gives the drink a more NATURAL taste. Honestly, it's way better than sugar, to me.

Nigerian Fish Rolls

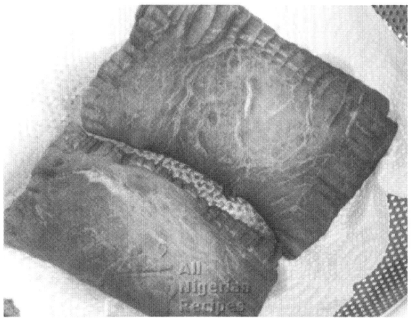

This is more of a famous snack in Nigeria, than a side dish. It's easy and quick to make.

Cook/prep time- 35 min

What you need:

- **2 ½ c Flour**
- **½ c butter- melted**
- **1 egg**
- **1 T baking powder**
- **½ T salt**
- **Extra virgin olive oil**

For the filling:

- **1 can of sardines**
- **½ T chili powder**
- **¼ t onion powder**
- **1 T curry (optional)**
- **½ T olive oil**
- **⅓ t basil**
- **⅓ t turmeric**

What to do:

Whisk the egg in a small bowl. Set aside

In a large bowl, mix the flour, salt, baking powder and margarine. Mix it around, then add the egg and mix again.

As you keep on mixing, slowly add some water, until you get a nice smooth, but firm dough. Set aside.

In another bowl, mash the sardines well with a fork. Add the chili powder, onion powder, curry, olive oil, basil and turmeric. Mix well.

Now, lay the dough on a flat surface. Roll out until it's flat and then cut it, so that it forms a rectangular shape.

Now add the mashed fish and fold the dough over the fish, and seal the ends by pressing the fork through the dough, like you would a pie crust.

Heat the oil to medium hot and fry the fish squares for about 10 to 12 minutes or until the crust is golden. Have it with the Tea-monade, or even hot tea and enjoy!

Eat n' Play

Although this may sound like a 'childish' name for a chapter, it pertains to everyone: kids, teens, and adults. Eating healthy isn't the only factor that'll help you maintain a healthy lifestyle; it's only a part of it. The other factor is exercise. Yes, I said the dreaded word: exercise!

So many people today have trouble with exercising and staying fit. Not exercising once a day, or at minimum a few times a week, is a recipe for an unhealthy life. Even if it's something as simple as doing jumping jacks or 15 minutes of aerobics, you have got to do **something!** Had it not been for Phys. Ed. in school which was required exercise, I'm positive I would've gained weight over the years; but even that little bit of exercise kept me in shape.

The bottom line is if you want to lose weight, stay fit, and stay healthy, you have to start eating healthy and exercising *daily.* There's no way around it. We have to stop convincing ourselves that there is, because there's not! I apologize if I come off a little harsh, but I just want everyone to get the point.

If you really want to get fit, and be healthy, all it's going to take is a little *commitment.* Let me give you a perfect example of commitment and something I witness every day. For the past 2 months, I have seen one of my neighbors, exercise consistently every single day; I'm talking about every single day. I would see her bright and early in the morning; by at least 6: 30 / 7: 00 she would be up, and jogging around the block multiple times for at least an hour. Then again at noon, and in the evening. That takes commitment. I don't really know the person, but every time I see her passing by, a smile comes to my face because I think what she does is a wonderful thing, and I can't help but think that she has mastered the art of self- discipline. If we could only develop that sort of commitment, there's no telling where we would be in life!

Now, I've devised a little plan that I think will keep us active. A simple routine that I like to call "Eat n' Play" (the title basically gives it away). Here's the concept. You take in calories, you burn it off; that simple. One of the ways you stay healthy is by burning off the excess calories you consume.

I've been following this routine for the last couple of months, and I can see the results already. I even see changes in places where I never thought would be affected. I noticed that my skin is looking much healthier, and that the little acne that I had disappeared (from the reduction of sugar consumption). I'm sure that if it works for me, it'll work for you.

Here's the routine you should follow:

At least 2-3 days a week, try to work on the major muscle groups by doing.

- Bicep curls, pushups, ab curls, bench press, shoulder press, squats, pull ups, sprinting, rowing, tug of war, jump rope, climbing hills or steps

At least 2 or more days a week, work on your flexibility by doing...

- Side jumps, step stretch, hurdler stretch, calf stretch, yoga stretches, torso stretch, torso twist, neck stretch, quadriceps stretch, hamstring stretch

At least 3-5 days every week, do some aerobic exercises by...

- Bike riding, brisk walking, running, dancing, trampoline, playground activities (for kids), basketball, jogging, jumping jacks, swimming, tennis

Every day, fit in some moderately physical activities like...

- Walking, climbing stairs, gardening/ yard work (great for the kids), house cleaning (also great), low- impact aerobics, handball, playing catch, swinging

Imagine the results if you were to follow such an easy routine for just 30 minutes a day! If you want to go longer, then congrats to you. But remember, in the end it'll be you who gets affected. But really, close your eyes for about 15 seconds and think of the benefits you would reap from putting in that one hour.

Here is what America struggles with. We have the guidelines, the steps, and the rules we need to follow in order to maintain a healthy lifestyle. Instead of following it, we like to contort those rules in our own way so that it fits with how we like it. There are a whole lot of complaints about obesity statistics, and no action is being taken to stop the amount of junk we eat, and the crazy amount of hours spent doing NOTHING. We have the answers, but we're not using them. Listen to this:

Did you know that the average American watches a little more than 4 hours of TV per day, 28 hours per week, which translates to 2 months of non-stop TV per year!? Imagine yourself sitting in front the TV for two months straight, nonstop. You see how absurd that is!? The average youth spends 900 hours in school per year, and **1500** hours watching TV per year. Now tell me we don't have a problem! It's all this TV watching, video-game playing, Internet surfing, phone using hours that contribute to the obesity in America. And people ask why we're so obese. There's your answer!

It is possible to do this, and it can be fun. Just have to decide that it's going to be fun, and don't look at it as strenuous work. I give you my Word, the only thing a man has, that this will produce positive outcomes.

Save $, Eat Better!

I decided to add this section on because I think you would benefit from it. Times are hard now, and the economy is not in our favor. Money is tight, and people have less and less to spend. So, I thought I would mention a few ways to save money, while in the kitchen. It's a great thing to be able to save money, while in the kitchen.

1) Eat at Home

It amazes me how I hear from some people about the amount of times they eat out. In times like this, people shouldn't be wasting money eating at restaurants, and ordering takeout (all the time). First of all it's not healthy, and second of all it's a waste of money, when you could make an inexpensive, easy, 30 minute meal at home. Save your money, and stop eating out all the time (for those of you this may apply to).   The good thing about eating at home is you get to spend some time with the kids or your wife, or parents. Gather them around the table, and indulge them in a little conversation.

2) Leftovers!

People have so many left over items in their fridge that can be used to make a quick and easy meal, it's unbelievable. Things like left over rotisserie chicken, rice, ground beef or turkey meat, tuna, or anything of that sort you could use to make meals like chicken salad or chicken soup, the Festive Fried Rice, Personal Chicken Salad, pasta with meat sauce, tuna salad, (just to name a few) without having to spend money and buy fresh produce to make a brand new meal, when you practically have one sitting right under your nose. Just take the time out to see what you have, and what could be done with it. The creativity happens when you make something of it.

3) Pre- made items = Convenience

A good way to save money and time is to sometimes buy things that are pre- made. Doing this could potentially save you time, and of course time is money. For example, for the strawberry shortcake recipe, I listed Pillsbury biscuits as one of the ingredients because instead of having to make your own, you can just pop those in the oven, and continue on, cutting the cooking time drastically.

4) One Night stand

Are you the type to make a meal to eat for one night, and that's it? Or perhaps the type to not cook all the chicken in a pack, because it's "too much" to make? I used to do that all the time. It's a waste, actually. It makes more sense to do it all in one sitting, so that you wouldn't have to come back the next day and spend unnecessary time cooking the same thing again, or spending money making something different, or even wasting money on gas because you have to finish the chicken you opened up before it goes bad. Doing it at once, you'll have none of that to worry about, plus there's leftovers!

5) Think ahead!

Say you're making dinner, and you remember you'll need to make lunch to bring to work tomorrow too. Wouldn't it be wise to make a little extra so that you can pack some away for tomorrow's lunch at the office, so that way you won't have to worry about running to McDonalds for a #6 to have for lunch?

There are plenty of ways to save money, all it requires is a little thought, creativity.

<u>*Dr. Oz's Power Foods*</u>

I am a fan of Dr. Oz. A big fan. And nowadays, his advice on how to live a healthier lifestyle is like gold! So I thought it would be nice to include some of what he calls "Power Foods". These are foods that are sure to increase your health. Try them; seriously, try them. And see the positive results for yourself.

Black Soybeans- According to Dr. Oz, Black Soybeans actually have more proteins and antioxidants than any other bean. And the cool thing about Black Soybeans is that they have very few carbs, which means they take longer for the body to digest, which means they help you to stay "fuller" longer, so you won't be tempted to snack on junk food.

Turmeric- Turmeric is actually a spice that helps give Curry its flavor; it's an antioxidant, an antiseptic, and has properties that prevent inflammation. Curcumin, a compound found in Turmeric that gives it its color, is known to help prevent Cancer, Alzheimer's disease, and helps with blood circulation. (Found in the ginger Curry Chicken)

Coconut Oil- Becoming more and more popular, Coconut Oil can help to shield your body from bacteria and viruses, help to control blood sugar levels, lower cholesterol, assist with food digestion, and even maintain a healthy weight balance. (Found in the Sautéed Spinach)

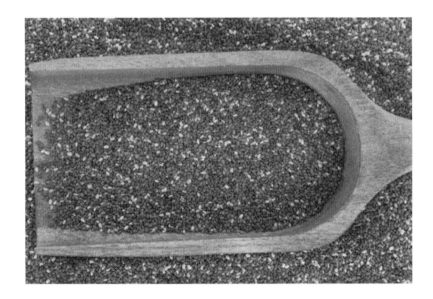

Chia Seeds- Just like Black Soybeans, Chia Seeds provide a lot of antioxidants, vitamins, minerals, and fiber. The cool thing about these seeds is that, according to Dr. Oz, they contain 500% more Calcium than milk, and it has the same amount of Omega- 3 as wild Salmon.

Cocoa- Cocoa actually has way more benefits than people think. It contains large amounts of ***Flavonoids***, a natural chemical in plants that helps fight against strokes, diabetes, and heart disease, and can even help lower blood pressure. It also contains compounds that help boost Serotonin & Endorphins, two chemicals that help us to feel happy. [http://bit.ly/ISjjGV- Pharrell's "Happy" Song :p]

Lingonberries- This berry almost looks like a mix between a cherry and a mini pomegranate. But it sure packs a punch. They help the body fight diabetes and cancer, they help prevent bad cholesterol, heart attacks, and strokes. Studies have shown that these berries can replace antioxidants that protect our nerve tissue and lower any potential damage to the body from inflammation.

Eggs- Despite what everyone says, the yolks of eggs is where the most minerals, calcium, and vitamins come from. Apparently, eggs are so rich with nutrients, that scientists have reported that a few eggs a day can provide more vitamins than a multivitamin. They also contain huge amounts of protein and something called *Carotenoids* which is good for maintaining healthy eyes.

Mustard Greens- On the Greek island of Icaria, 1 in 3 people live to see 90 years. Why is that? Because Mustard Greens is one of their diet staples. It's rich in Vitamin k. Not only that, it contains something called **Sulforaphanes** that help the body get rid of bile acid (an acid found in your gut; it's also used to create cholesterol). Getting rid of that bile acid means cutting your cholesterol.

Beet Juice- Ever wonder what gives Beets its distinct red color? It's a "cancer- fighting antioxidant" called **Belatin**. Besides that, Belatin also helps to protect the liver, and it dilates the body's blood vessels, allowing blood to flow easier.

TIP: Cooking Beets actually reduces the chance of your body absorbing all the vitamins, so it's best to juice them.

Sweet Potatoes- My favorite! For some reason, the women in Okinawa, Japan are ranked as some of the longest living women. It could be attributed to the fact that they eat a sweet potato called "Limo" every day with breakfast, lunch and dinner. Did you know that sweet potatoes have high levels if beta- carotene, Vitamin A, and Vitamin C? Or that they have 150% more antioxidants than blueberries. Sweet potatoes have the ability to help maintain a strong immune system.

My Favorite Chefs

After the couple hundred recipes I've gone through, I always mark the ones I like, that stand out to me, and the ones I have tried. I thought you might like to try them out for yourself, and get creative with them if you like. Here are my top 5.

From *Willie Crawford:*

Salmon Croquettes

Ingredients:

- 1 12 oz can pink salmon
- 2 Whole eggs
- 1/4 cup chopped onion
- 1/4 cup all-purpose flour
- 2 tablespoons yellow corn meal
- 1/2 teaspoon salt (depending upon the brand and how much salt is in it you can leave this out if you want.
- 1/2 teaspoon ground black pepper

You basically pour all of the ingredients into a large bowl and mix them. A large spoon or a potato masher worked fine. I add the flour last because I sometimes adjust the amount to control the consistency. Mold the dough-like mix that you end up with into patties (like thick homemade hamburgers).

Coat a frying pan with a little cooking oil. Crisco works just fine. Preheat the oiled pan over medium heat. Slip the patties into the pan, fitting as many as you can but leaving room to turn them. Cook until medium brown on one side, then turn over and do the same to the other side.

Willie's Famous Cookbook – http://amzn.to/1p7EvcO

From *Rachael Ray*:

CREAMY BLT PASTA

Rach tops penne with a sauce simmered with bacon.

Leeks burst fresh tomatoes and cheese.

INGREDIENTS

- Salt
- 1 pound penne *or* other short-cut pasta with lines
- 2 tablespoons extra virgin olive oil (EVOO)
- 5-6 slices lean, thick-cut good quality bacon, sliced across into 1/2-inch thick sticks
- 3 medium leeks, trimmed, halved lengthwise and sliced 1/2-inch thick
- 3-4 cloves garlic, thinly sliced
- Black pepper
- 1 round tablespoon tomato paste
- 1/2 cup dry white wine
- 1 pint cherry tomatoes
- 1 package Boursin cheese (5.4 ounces) *or* 1/2 cup crème fraiche combined with 3 tablespoons minced mixed herbs, such as thyme, sage, rosemary and parsley
- Grated Parmigiano Reggiano cheese

Bring a large pot of water to a boil for the pasta. Once at a full rolling boil, salt the water and cook pasta to al dente.

Meanwhile, heat 1 tablespoon EVOO (Extra Virgin Olive Oil), one turn of the pan, over medium-high heat. Add the bacon and brown to crisp. Remove from the pan and reserve. Add the leeks and garlic and season with pepper. Stir for a few minutes to soften, then add the tomato paste and stir for a minute more; add the wine and reduce by half. Add the tomatoes and put a lid on the pot. Let the tomatoes burst, about 8-10 minutes. Stir in the cheese; reduce heat to low.

Reserve about 1/2 cup of the starchy cooking water just before draining pasta, then drain and add the pasta to the sauce. Add the bacon back in and toss, using the starchy cooking water to combine. Adjust the seasoning of pasta, to taste; serve in shallow bowls topped with the cheese and garnished with the tomatoes.

My favorite Rachael Cookbook- http://amzn.to/1n50i5v

From *Chef Bobby Flay*:

Chinese Chicken Salad with Red Chile Peanut Dressing

Ingredients

- 1/4 cup rice wine vinegar
- 2 tablespoons smooth peanut butter
- 1 tablespoon chopped fresh ginger
- 2 teaspoons chipotle pepper puree
- 1 tablespoon soy sauce
- 1 tablespoon honey
- 2 teaspoons toasted sesame oil
- 1/2 cup canola oil
- Salt and freshly ground pepper
- 1/2 head Napa cabbage, shredded
- 1/2 head romaine lettuce, shredded
- 2 carrots, shredded
- 1/4 pound snow peas, julienned
- 1/4 cup coarsely chopped fresh cilantro leaves
- 1/4 cup thinly sliced green onion
- 2 cups shredded rotisserie chicken
- 1/2 cup chopped roasted peanuts
- 1/4 cup chopped fresh mint leaves
- Chili oil, optional
- Grilled lime halves, for garnish

Whisk together the vinegar, peanut butter, ginger, chipotle pepper puree, soy sauce, honey, sesame oil, and canola oil in a medium bowl. Season with salt and pepper, to taste. Combine cabbage, lettuce, carrots, snow peas, cilantro, and green onion in a large bowl. Add the dressing and toss to combine.

Transfer to a serving platter and top with the shredded chicken, chopped peanuts, and mint. Drizzle with chili oil, if desired. Garnish with grilled lime halves.

One of Bobby's Best Sellers

Favorite Bobbly Flay Cookbook- http://amzn.to/1zXxDEw

From *Jamie Oliver*:

Delicious roasted white fish wrapped in smoked bacon with lemon mayonnaise and asparagus

Ingredients

- 4 x 200g white fish fillets, cut 2.5cm thick, skinned and pin boned
- 2 sprigs of fresh rosemary, leaves picked and very finely chopped
- zest and juice of 2 lemons
- Freshly ground black pepper
- 16 rashers of thinly sliced, smoked streaky bacon or pancetta
- Olive oil
- 4 tablespoons mayonnaise
- 2 large bunches of asparagus, trimmed

Preheat your oven to 200ºC/400ºF/gas 6. Season your beautiful fish filets with the rosemary, finely grated lemon zest (no bitter white pith, please) and pepper – you don't need to use salt because we're going to wrap the fish in the lovely salty smoked bacon. Lay your rashers of bacon or pancetta on a board and one by one run the flat of a knife along them to thin them and widen them out. Lay 4 rashers together, slightly overlapping, put a fish filet on top and wrap the rashers around it.

Lightly heat a large ovenproof frying pan, add a splash of olive oil and lay your fish, prettiest side facing up, in the pan. Fry for a minute, then place the pan in your preheated oven for 10 to 12 minutes, depending on the thickness of the fish, until the bacon is crisp and golden.

While the fish is cooking, you can make your simple lemon mayonnaise. I do this by mixing homemade mayonnaise with a nice amount of lemon juice and pepper. Or, if you'd rather sit down for five minutes with a glass of wine, use some ready-made mayo instead! You want to add enough lemon juice to make the flavor slightly too zingy. This is because, when you eat it with the asparagus and the fish, it will lessen slightly in intensity. And don't worry if the mayo looks a little thinner than usual when you've added the lemon juice – think of it as more delicate.

The asparagus is a great accompaniment because, like the fish, it also loves bacon. You can either boil or steam it; either way it's light and a nice contrast to the meatiness of the fish. When cooked, toss it in the juices that come out of the fish. Simply serve the fish next to a nice pile of asparagus, drizzled with the lemon-spiked mayonnaise. And if you're feeling very hungry, serve with some steaming-hot new potatoes.

Jamie's Healthy Eating Cookbook- http://amzn.to/1u87JgR

From *Chef G. Garvin*:

Bourbon-marinated skirt steak deluxe

Ingredients

- 1 cup soy sauce
- 1/2 cup finely chopped red onion
- 1/4 cup packed brown sugar
- 1/4 cup Worcestershire sauce
- 1/4 cup bourbon
- 2 Tablespoon chopped shallots
- 2 Tablespoons chopped garlic
- 1 Tablespoon olive oil
- 1 teaspoon dry mustard
- Kosher salt
- Coarsely ground black pepper
- 2 8-ounce pieces beef skirt steak
- 1/2 cup (1 stick) unsalted butter, softened
- 1 teaspoon dried parsley flakes
- 4 6-inch Cuban rolls or 4 Kaiser Rolls- split
- 2 large heirloom tomatoes, sliced
- 16 slices mozzarella cheese

For marinade, in a bowl whisk together soy sauce, red onion, brown sugar, Worcestershire sauce, bourbon, shallots, 1 tablespoon of garlic, the olive oil, mustard, a pinch of salt and a pinch of black pepper. Place meat in a re-sealable plastic bag. Marinate in refrigerator for at least 30 minutes or up to 1 hour turning occasionally.

Meanwhile, preheat broiler. In a small bowl whip together butter and remaining 1 Tablespoon garlic, the parsley, a pinch of salt, and a pinch of pepper. Spread butter mixture on cut sides of rolls. Place rolls, buttered sides up on a baking sheet. Broil for 1 to 2 minutes or until edges of the rolls start to brown. Remove from broiler; set aside.

Remove meat from marinade; discard marinade. Place meat on the rack of the uncovered grill directly over medium coals. Grill about 8 minutes or until medium doneness (160°F), turning once. Remove from grill; let stand 5 minutes to cool slightly, thinly slice meat diagonally across the grain.

Divide meat slices among roll bottoms. Top each sandwich with some of the tomato slices. Add four slices of mozzarella cheese to each sandwich. Return to broiler; broil for 1 to 2 minutes or until cheese is melted and bubbly. Top sandwiches with roll tops. Cut in half and serve.

One of G's famous cookbooks- I REALLY like this one- http://amzn.to/1naEbdj

Afterword

Writing this book did take a lot of work, effort, patience, and time. Not to mention how often I got "writers block." I spent a lot of time sitting at the computer staring at a blank screen, it seems as though I could've written another book, but I'm pleased with this one.

This is just the first, out of many more, to come. Like I said in the intro, my biggest hope is that this book helped you, somehow. I'm glad that I can share some of what I've learned. I've been taught good things, and it feels awesome to be able to share them. This book isn't about just me trying to earn money for college; it's about me trying to help someone. After all of this I must say I learned a few lessons, some of which are: never be closed minded and when you are given a good idea, run with it.

Remember in the intro I said my Mom gave me the idea of doing an e-book, and "after giving it some thought I decided it was a good idea"? Yeah, well, I had thoughts of opposition. I was literally thinking "Oohh mannn, I am NOT trying to spend my summer writing a book!!"

I immediately thought of it as "too much work" and I don't "feel" like doing it.

But that was the problem. I was turned off by the thought of the amount of work it would take to complete, and I had a closed minded attitude about it. This stumbling block is what can stop some REALLY nice ideas from coming to fruition. Just imagine, these hindrances could even stop someone from becoming a potential million, or billionaire.

Where would we be right now if Henry Ford got the idea for the assembly line, but decided "nahhhh, I don't feel like doing it. Too much work." I'm telling you, we would not be where we are today, that's for sure.

I must admit, it's something I have struggled with, but luckily I seem to be turning a corner, and I'm happy about that.

If you know of someone who struggles with being close minded and is turned off by the amount of "work" putting great ideas into action might take, or even if you struggle with this, I encourage you to try to overcome it. It can be limiting, and you will never know what you're truly capable of, or how many people you can help. To get over that mindset, just take action – a little bit each day, and do the work, so you/others can enjoy the results!

And to all the youth/ teens/ college students reading this...hear me out. If I can do this, so can you. Learn to be self-sufficient; learn to be able to rely on yourself to do things your parents would normally have to do for you. You don't know how much of a blessing it would be for your mom or dad or whoever it may be, to know that "my son/ daughter got this. I don't need to worry." And another thing, If you have ever had an idea, or a dream, or something that you wanted to pursue, or some cool idea that you thought about that you know would benefit others, I encourage you to DO IT. The world is in desperate need of young people with bright, new, and innovative ideas.

It's been a blast writing this book, and I hope you enjoyed it. I can't thank you enough for all of your support. You are a blessing, and I sincerely thank you.

Christian Kelly

17105278R00053

Printed in Great Britain
by Amazon